The Wise Girl

Joan Aiken

Illustrated by Emma Garner

OXFORD
UNIVERSITY PRESS

Once upon a time a shepherd found a golden pot buried in a wood. He told his daughter that he was going to take it to the King.

"Don't do that," said his daughter, who was called Regina.

"Why not?" he asked.

"Because if you do, he will only ask for the spoon that goes with it. Then you will be in trouble."

But the father didn't listen to his daughter. He took the pot to the King, who instantly demanded the spoon as well, just as the girl had said.

"Bring it to me, or you will be in trouble," he said.
The shepherd began to groan and cry. "My
daughter was right! I should have listened to her. She
told me that when you had got the bowl you would
want the spoon as well," he said.

The King was interested. He said, "Tell me about your daughter."

"Oh, she is a very clever girl, your Majesty. She can tell a boiled egg from a raw egg just by looking at it."

"Well," said the King, "tell her to come to me this evening neither clothed nor unclothed, neither walking nor riding, neither speaking nor silent. If I like her I will marry her and make her Queen. And I won't ask for the golden spoon."

The shepherd went home very worried. But Regina remained perfectly calm.

When dusk fell, she went to the King all dressed in fishing nets. She took a large goat and partly she rode on it, partly she walked and all the way to the king she hummed a tune, neither speaking nor silent.

The King said to her, "Regina, what can be heard at the farthest distance?"

Regina said, "Thunder and a lie can be heard at the farthest distance."

Then the King stroked his long, bushy beard and said, "Regina, can you guess what my beard is worth?"

Regina said, "No need to guess. Your Majesty's beard is worth three summers. It has taken three years to grow."

The King was astonished, and said, "She guessed right! Nobody else knew that."

The King saw that Regina was indeed as clever as her father had made her out to be.

So he said, "Regina, you shall be my wife. But you must not give advice to anybody, not to me nor to a single soul in the whole wide world. If you give advice to anybody, we shall have to part. Do you agree?"

Regina thought about it. Then she said, "It shall be so. But will your Majesty write this promise in your own hand on a piece of paper – that if we ever part, I may take with me from the palace the one thing I like best?"

The King saw no harm in that, so he wrote his promise on a piece of paper. Regina took it, and was careful to keep it always pinned on her shawl.

So the King and Regina were married, and lived together happily. And she gave advice to nobody.

Now, one day it happened that the King was outside his palace when he heard two women quarrelling loudly.

"What is the matter with you two women?" asked the King.

"Her child threw dust at my child, so I boxed his ears," said the first woman.

"She had no right to box my son's ears," said the second woman.

"Her child is an ill-behaved brat," said the first woman.

"Just the same, you had no right to box his ears," said the King.

The first woman turned and spat at the King. So he had her thrown into prison. But then he began to worry.

"After all," he thought, "this is a very small affair. People will laugh at me for making so much of it. But then, the King should be treated with respect. What should I do?"

In his trouble he went to Regina. He told her the whole story, and asked her what she thought.

Regina said, "Never carry a cow up a tree. Never look for honey in a salt mine. Never offer advice to a mother about her child. You should let the woman out of prison, telling her that she has been punished enough for her rudeness."

"What about the other woman whose boy threw dust? Should I punish her?" asked the King.

Regina said, "The boy will grow up to be her punishment. You need do nothing more."

The King decided that Regina was right, and he did as she suggested.

Then he remembered her promise. He said to her, "You have given advice although I warned you not to. You must leave me tomorrow. But you may take from the palace the thing that you like best."

Regina knew there would be no point in arguing or making a fuss. So she ordered a splendid banquet for all the King's lords and ladies to say goodbye to them.

Late into the night they feasted and sang. Regina wore her old dress of fishing nets, which she had covered with silver.

When the feast was nearly over, she brought a glass of wine to the King and said, "You must drink this to my health."

Regina had put a sleeping potion into the wine and when the King had drunk it, he fell into a deep sleep.

Next morning, when the carriage came to take Regina back to their father's hut, the King was still asleep.

Regina told her servants to pick him up and put him in the carriage. Then, when they arrived at her father's hut, she and her father took the King out of the carriage. They laid him on a bed of straw, where he went on sleeping for many hours.

When the King woke up he looked around him,
astonished, and asked where he was.

"Who brought me here?" he asked.
"I did," said Regina.
"How did you dare to do such a thing?" he cried.

"Didn't you write down on a bit of paper that I
could take from the palace the thing that I loved best?"
And she showed him the piece of paper.

The King saw his name on the piece of paper. He laughed and kissed Regina. So they drove back to the palace again. And from that day, the King often asked his wife's advice, and she often gave it.